Mysterious Encounters

The Bermuda Triangle

by Katy S. Duffield

KIDHAVEN PRESS

A part of Gale, Cengage Learning

GALE
CENGAGE Learning

Detroit • New York • San Francisco • New Haven, Conn • Waterville, Maine • London

LIBRARY OF CONGRESS CATALOGING-IN-PUBLICATION DATA

Duffield, Katy.
   The Bermuda Triangle / by Katy S. Duffield.
      p. cm. — (Mysterious encounters)
   Includes bibliographical references and index.
   ISBN 978-0-7377-4046-2 (hardcover)
   1. Bermuda Triangle—Juvenile literature. I. Title.
   G558.D84 2008
   001.94—dc22

                                                              2008002227

KidHaven Press
27500 Drake Rd
Farmington Hills MI 48331

ISBN-13: 978-0-7377-4046-2
ISBN-10: 0-7377-4046-9

Printed in the United States of America
1 2 3 4 5 6 7 12 11 10 09 08

Contents

Chapter 1

What Is the Bermuda Triangle?

On a clear night in June 2001, boaters Paul Vance and Doug Gerdon were out cruising off the eastern coast of Florida in Vance's sailboat, *Rare Form*. About 9:30 P.M. the men noticed a strange white light in the sky. Vance watched as "a swirling mist . . . engulfed the light [and] the light slowly drifted down into the mist." Vance reported that the light "descended through the mist tunnel and disappeared . . . [as if] the mist was a door."[1] At the exact time Vance and Gerdon saw the light, their boat's motor lost power. The men were alone and adrift on the ocean with only the stars to light their way.

The boaters were especially worried because they were well aware of their location. They were floating in a mysterious area known as the Bermuda Triangle. Fortunately for the boaters, an east wind allowed them to sail safely back to shore. After the unusual encounter, Vance said, "I'll have to admit . . . when the engine faltered and I saw that swirling mist, I thought to myself, there's something to this Bermuda Triangle stuff!"[2]

Triangle of Death?

Mysterious lights, unusual fog and mist, malfunctioning electronic equipment, vanishing ships, and

The area that makes up the Bermuda Triangle goes from Miami to Puerto Rico to Bermuda and back to Miami.

disappearing planes are only some of the mysterious **phenomena** that have reportedly occurred in this area of the western Atlantic Ocean. It was not until the 1960s when a journalist began looking into the numerous unexplained happenings in this area that the area received its name—the Bermuda Triangle. The Bermuda Triangle, also known as the "Devil's Triangle," the "Triangle of Death," and the "Hoodoo Sea," is located just off the southeastern coast of the United States. If an imaginary line were drawn from Miami, Florida, to Puerto Rico, to Bermuda, and back to Miami, this line would roughly outline the area that is considered the Bermuda Triangle.

Perhaps one of the most intriguing details of the Triangle is that planes, ships, and boats have been reported lost without a trace in the area. In many cases, no wreckage was found and often no distress

Another Triangle?

Some sources say a Bermuda Triangle–like area, dubbed the Dragon's Triangle, lurks in the Pacific Ocean off the coast of Japan. Missing ships and planes and compass and mechanical abnormalities have been noted in this area.

calls were made prior to the losses. Investigators are astonished that entire planes and ships, along with their crews and passengers, could simply vanish with no sign that they had ever existed. Many investigators have studied these cases searching for scientific explanations for the disappearances. It is impossible to calculate the exact number of ships, planes, and lives that have been lost in the Triangle over the years, but many researchers estimate that thousands of aircraft and vessels have gone missing there.

Columbus's Experiences in the Triangle

As far back as the time of Christopher Columbus, sailors have reported unexplained happenings within the area now known as the Bermuda Triangle. According to author Charles Berlitz, Columbus wrote in his logbook that while sailing in an area of the Triangle known as the Sargasso Sea, he witnessed "a huge bolt of fire shoot[ing] across the heavens."[3] Later, Columbus and his crew were said to have grown alarmed when their compass produced incorrect readings. Instead of pointing toward true north, the compass was off by several degrees. During Columbus's time, the compass was the primary tool used to keep ships on course, so this malfunction added an extra eeriness to the fire bolt Columbus had observed.

The Sargasso Sea is a region of the Atlantic Ocean that was unlike anything Columbus and his

Unexplained happenings in the Bermuda Triangle go as far back as the time of Christopher Columbus.

men had seen before. There is very little wind or ocean current within this area of the North Atlantic, so the surface remains quite calm. During Columbus's time, sailors relied on the wind and ocean currents to propel them toward their destinations. Since the Sargasso Sea lacked both, sailors sometimes became stranded until the breeze picked up enough to thrust them on their way. Myths of long ago claim that, at times, ships remained stranded for such long periods that a crew's food and water supplies would run out, causing the crew to die of thirst or starvation.

Along with calm waters, the Sargasso carries with it another distinctive feature. Huge masses of seaweed cover the water's surface—something not often seen in the open ocean. **Superstitious** sailors who sailed even before Columbus's time believed that sea monsters lived within the seaweed and occasionally emerged from the thick mass to devour unsuspecting ships and their crews. Stories such as these helped the Bermuda Triangle gain its peculiar and deadly reputation.

Myth or Reality?

Hundreds of years have passed since Columbus's voyage into the Bermuda Triangle, but the mystery of the Triangle still survives. Almost every year planes, boats, and ships are reported lost or missing in the Bermuda Triangle. On the night of December 22, 1967, two friends set out from Miami on the cabin cruiser *Witchcraft*. The men were off to enjoy an evening of viewing onshore Christmas lights from their boat. After traveling only about a mile offshore, one of the men radioed the Seventh District Coast Guard office in Miami to ask for assistance. The boat's propeller had struck an underwater object and it needed to be towed to shore. Fewer than twenty minutes later, the Coast Guard arrived at the designated location but was unable to find any trace of the

Some reports of missing planes and boats in the Bermuda Triangle can be explained but others seem to have no explanation.

men or the boat. A 1,200-square-mile (3,108sq.-km) search turned up nothing.

In 1978 Eastern Caribbean flight 912 was preparing to land in good weather at the St. Thomas airport. According to air traffic controller William Kittenger, when the plane was "two miles out, I had visual contact,"[4] but when Kittenger checked the radar again, the plane was gone. Kittenger immediately notified the Coast Guard, which, in turn, began a search. According to authorities, if the plane crashed where Kittenger had last seen it, the wreckage should have been easily located in an area of shallow water, but it was not. No debris from the plane was ever recovered and no survivors were ever found.

Many researchers dismiss the idea that there is anything odd or unexplained going on in the area of the Bermuda Triangle. These researchers believe that human error, strong storms, or mechanical failure is to blame for the accidents. They also believe that no more boat, ship, or plane accidents occur in this area than in other geographical areas. The U.S. Coast Guard does not recognize the name "Bermuda Triangle" and according to its Web site, "there has been nothing discovered that

Fueling the Fire

In a May 2006 British newspaper, a headline read: "Monsters From Beneath the Bermuda Triangle." Instead of monsters, readers learned that researchers had discovered microscopic animals called zooplankton in the waters of the Bermuda Triangle. Headlines such as these only serve to fuel the mystery that surrounds the Bermuda Triangle.

would indicate that casualties were the result of anything other than physical causes. No extraordinary factors have ever been identified."[5]

Even though many people believe there are logical explanations for the losses that take place in the area known as the Bermuda Triangle, there are plenty more who remain convinced that something unexplainable and out of the ordinary is going on there. Since no survivors were found in many of these accidents, investigators often have few clues to help them determine the actual cause of the disappearances. This fact only adds to the Bermuda Triangle mystique.

Chapter 2

Vanishing Ships and Crews

As all sailors know, the ocean can be a powerful and destructive force. Rapidly forming thunderstorms, giant waves, **waterspouts**, and hurricanes can have deadly effects on ships and boats at sea. Fortunately for modern-day sailors, most oceangoing ships and boats are fitted with the latest technological advances such as satellite weather radar and a **global positioning system (GPS)** to help them navigate the huge expanses of ocean on which they travel. This was not always the case, however. Throughout the years, numerous boats and ships have been lost in the Bermuda Triangle. The wreckage of some of the vessels has been located on the ocean floor, while other vessels

A massive ocean whirlpool could swallow a ship whole.

seem to have vanished without a trace. Still other ships have been found completely intact, drifting peacefully on the ocean current, yet deserted of passengers and crew. Poor weather conditions or other factors can be blamed for some of these incidents, but others seem unexplainable.

USS Cyclops

One of the most widely known Bermuda Triangle ship losses is that of a U.S. Navy ship, the *Cyclops*. In 1918 the *Cyclops* left port in Brazil headed for the east coast of the United States. The ship, which helped supply the military during World War I, carried a load of manganese and a crew of around 300. The *Cyclops* was a relatively new ship at only eight years old, was piloted by an experienced captain, and was fitted with a sophisticated radio system. No problems were expected on the voyage. But all that changed on March 4, 1918. After making a stop in Barbados, the *Cyclops* and her crew continued on their way. Some reports say, at that time, the ship headed south rather than north, which would have led it far off course. No one knows what happened next—the ship was never seen or heard from again.

When the *Cyclops* was overdue for its return, the U.S. Navy immediately began an investigation and

The mysterious disappearance of the *Cyclops* is one of the most widely known Bermuda Triangle losses.

Turning Turtle

Anything from structural problems and shifting cargo loads to hurricanes and huge waves can cause a ship to turn upside down, or capsize. When a ship flips completely over, sailors say that it has "turned turtle."

sent out search teams. There had been some reports of bad weather occurring at the time the ship disappeared, but a ship as large and as sturdy as the *Cyclops* should not have been affected. The ship, over 500 feet (152m) long and weighing more than 19,000 tons (17,237 metric tons), should have been able to withstand the reported weather conditions. Additional theories about the ship's fate include a report that she may have been struck by a German torpedo, or that the cargo she carried may have shifted, causing the ship to sink, but none of those theories was ever confirmed.

The most unusual aspect about the disappearance is the fact that no distress call, or **SOS**, was reported and search crews found absolutely no wreckage or debris. It seems impossible that a ship of that size could have vanished without leaving anything behind. After an exhaustive investigation, Navy officials stated, "The disappearance of this ship has been one of the most baffling mysteries in the annals of the Navy."[6] And the commander in chief at that time, President Woodrow Wilson, was quoted as saying, "Only God and the sea know what happened to the great ship."[7]

Intact Ships—Lost Crews

The *Cyclops* is not the only ship to mysteriously disappear while traveling in the Bermuda Triangle. It is impossible to say how many ships have been lost in the area throughout history, but according to author Gian J. Quasar, unknown factors cause the loss of about 60 boats in the Triangle each year. To add even more mystery and intrigue, several stories

When the *Mary Celeste* was found drifting in the Bermuda Triangle, there was no sign of the ship's captain or crew.

have been reported about ships that have been found floating completely intact within the Triangle, but with no trace of passengers or crew. In many of these cases, officials have no idea what changed these once-inhabited vessels into nothing more than ghost ships or **derelicts**.

One of the most famous ghost ships is the *Mary Celeste*. In the winter of 1872 while piloting his ship, the *Dei Gratia*, Captain Moorhouse noticed the *Mary Celeste* floating aimlessly near the Azores islands. Upon closer investigation, Captain Moor-

Accounts of tugboats hauling barges or damaged ships back to shore from the Bermuda Triangle are common.

house discovered that the *Mary Celeste* was adrift on its own—completely deserted of its passengers and crew. Although some of the ship's sails were partially torn, the ship appeared to be in good condition and plenty of food and water was found aboard. According to some reports, when Moorhouse boarded the *Mary Celeste*, he found a warm meal still sitting upon the stove as if it were about to be served. Toys were scattered about as if a child had recently finished playing with them. Nothing appeared to be amiss on the ship except for the fact that there was no life on board. The captain's log had not been written in for over a week, and his last entry gave no indication of any problems. No one knows what happened to the *Mary Celeste*'s captain, his wife, their young daughter, or the crew of eight men. Like many others, this abandoned ghost ship remains a mystery of the Bermuda Triangle.

Tugboat Tales

Along with derelict ships, some amazing stories from the Bermuda Triangle are also told about tugboats that haul barges or broken-down ships back to shore. One of the most interesting stories is that of the tug *Good News*. In 1966 Captain Don Henry and his crew were aboard *Good News* hauling a barge from Puerto Rico to Miami, Florida. Captain Henry was resting in his cabin when he heard some of his crewmen hollering loudly. When Henry went to see what was happening, his chief officer pointed to the tug's compass. According to Henry, "the magnetic compass was going completely bananas. It was simply going around and around. I had never seen anything like that before."[8]

The tug also had little power, no lights, and no radio communications. Henry glanced back to check the position of the barge they towed. A thick fog shrouded the barge so it was no longer visible. Henry gunned the engines and tried to get the tug moving, but it was as if "something was pulling us back. It was like being in the middle of a tug-o-war."[9] Eventually, Henry and his tug made their way out of the fog. When they did, the lights, radios, generators, and compasses began functioning normally again. Henry, an experienced seaman, is still unsure about what actually happened that day in the Bermuda Triangle, but he said, "it sure made me into a 'believer.'"[10]

Another frightening towing case involved Joe Talley and his fishing boat, *Wild Goose*, in 1944. Talley's boat had experienced engine trouble and had to be hauled in by the *Caicos Trader*. Talley dozed in his cabin as the *Wild Goose* was being towed. Suddenly, something unusual happened— the *Wild Goose* dove nose first into the ocean. The crew on the *Caicos Trader* watched in horror; they knew Talley was still aboard the *Wild Goose*. The pull of the water was so strong the *Caicos* crew's only choice was to cut the towline to the *Wild Goose*. If they had not, the *Caicos Trader* would

Vile Vortices

In a 1972 *Saga* magazine article titled "The Twelve Devils' Graveyards," investigator Ivan Sanderson put forth the theory that there are twelve evenly spaced areas throughout the world's oceans where unusual numbers of accidents have occurred. Sanderson believes these "vile vortices" of swirling ocean water have caused many ships to be lost.

have been pulled under as well. Amazingly, Talley was able to swim to the ocean's surface and was rescued by the crew of the *Caicos Trader.* Like many other boaters who have encountered strange situations in the Bermuda Triangle, Talley is not sure if he became trapped in an ocean whirlpool or if some other more mysterious factor contributed to his experience.

Chapter 3

Disappearing Planes

Ships are not the only form of transportation that have encountered bizarre and unusual circumstances in the waters of the Bermuda Triangle. The airspace above the Triangle carries its own share of mystery. Many airplane pilots and passengers have stories to tell about their remarkable adventures through the Triangle. From lost planes, to loss of radar contact, time warps, unusual fog or objects, and unexplained radio, electrical, and navigational problems, the Bermuda Triangle is well known for its disturbing aviation accounts. One such account took place on June 28, 1980, when José Maldonado Torres was flying to Puerto Rico with a friend. According to the flight transcript,

Torres radioed a distress call around 8:00 P.M. "**Mayday**, Mayday, We are lost. . . . Right now we are supposed to be about 35 miles from the coast of Puerto Rico but we have something weird in front of us that make[s] us lose our course all the time."[11] This was the last transmission from Torres. Shortly after this final radio contact, Torres's plane vanished from the radar screen. No wreckage or survivors were ever found.

The Lost Patrol

The case of flight 19 is perhaps the most famous disappearance of all that has occurred in the Bermuda Triangle. On December 5, 1945, not one, but five planes disappeared over the Triangle,

The five missing U.S. Navy TBM Avengers are the most famous casualties of the Bermuda Triangle.

and these were no ordinary planes—they were U.S. Navy bombers called TBM Avengers. The Avengers, flown by highly experienced pilots, took off in good weather conditions from Ft. Lauderdale, Florida, on what should have been a routine training mission. Almost two hours into the flight, the panicked flight leader called in to the tower "We can't find west. Everything is wrong. We can't be sure of any direction. Everything looks strange, even the ocean."[12] A few minutes later another transmission is received from a different pilot: "We can't tell where we are . . . everything is . . . can't make out anything. It looks like we are entering white water. . . . We're completely lost."[13]

Search and rescue boats and planes that were dispatched to the area found only clear skies and calm seas. There were no signs of debris, oil slicks, life rafts, or of any of the 27 airmen who had taken

---

Lost Patrol Found?

According to some reports in the early 1990s, a salvage company led by a group of deep-sea explorers believed they had discovered the wreckage of flight 19 in around 800 feet (244m) of water. It remains unclear if this is the actual wreckage of the Lost Patrol.

A C-119 "Flying Boxcar" disappeared in 1965 in the Bermuda Triangle despite good weather and no problems reported by the crew.

off from Ft. Lauderdale only hours earlier. Another layer of mystery was added to this tragedy when a Mariner rescue plane sent to search for the missing Avengers, and carrying a crew of thirteen, also disappeared without a trace.

An exhaustive search for the Avengers continued for a period of five days and covered an estimated 250,000 square miles (647,497sq. km) of the Atlantic Ocean and the Gulf of Mexico. No trace of the Avengers or of the rescue Mariner was ever found. One Navy board of inquiry investigator stated, "[The Avengers] vanished as completely as if they had flown to Mars."[14] It is impossible to say what actually happened to flight 19, which came to be known as the "Lost Patrol." Some people theorized that malfunctioning compasses caused the pilots to become disoriented or that the planes may have simply run out of fuel before making their way safely back to land.

Other Lost Planes

The exact number of planes that have been lost as they flew over the Bermuda Triangle is not known, but numerous reports have been filed over the years. Two particular planes of note were the sister planes the *Star Ariel* and the *Star Tiger*. These two luxury airliners shared similar fates in the skies over the Bermuda Triangle within one year of each other. In 1948 the *Star Tiger* left the Azores en route to Bermuda with 25 passengers and 6 crew members aboard. As the aircraft neared Bermuda, flight controllers received a radio transmission stating that all was well with the *Star Tiger*. That transmission was the final communication from the *Star Tiger* crew. Radio operators became alarmed when they did not hear back from the aircraft for a long period. Repeated attempts to contact those aboard failed.

A massive search to locate the plane and its passengers and crew ensued, but this search only prompted more mystery. During the search, radio operators along the Atlantic coast reported hearing the word *Tiger* spelled out by a rough form of

Morse code. In addition, reports say the Coast Guard in Newfoundland received the spoken message, "G-A-H-N-P."[15] These were the call letters of the *Star Tiger*.

One year later, the *Star Tiger*'s sister plane, the *Star Ariel*, left London for Chile. After a stop in Bermuda to refuel, the *Star Ariel* continued on its way. Like the *Star Tiger*, the *Star Ariel* reported no problems and sent out no distress calls, but this plane went missing as well. Both planes were flying in good weather and were in mechanically good condition, but neither plane made it to its final destination.

In 1965 a C-119 plane, called a flying boxcar due to its boxy shape, set off from Milwaukee, Wisconsin. The flight crew, members of Milwaukee's 440th Airlift Wing, was flying out to drop off supplies and

Many pilots have reported seeing a strange haze or fog while flying over the Bermuda Triangle.

crew members in the Bahamas, Puerto Rico, and the Dominican Republic. The weather conditions were good and no problems were reported from the crew, but something went wrong over the Atlantic that night. Radio traffic controllers became concerned when the flight was overdue for its return. Searches located nothing—no aircraft, no men, no debris. It was as if the plane simply vanished. One of the lost crewmen's wives, Phyllis Adams, studied the accident report and could not believe what she was being told. She said, "Let me put it this way: That was a big aircraft. There were ten people aboard. They had another engine on board. There was luggage. You mean to tell me that if that plane crashed that nothing was found? I don't buy it, I will never buy it."[16]

A Strange "Electronic Fog"

Along with compass abnormalities and planes that seem to simply vanish into thin air, there have been many reports of pilots flying through a strange haze or fog while cruising the airspace over the Bermuda Triangle. The difference in these cases is that many of these pilots lived to tell about the bizarre incidents they encountered. According to one report, pilot and author Martin Caidin, who flew from Bermuda to Florida in 1986, said, "The perfect weather disappeared . . . [we] could only see the nose right in front . . . the wingtips disappeared into what looked like the inside of a milk bottle. . . . You looked up, you saw a tiny patch of sky; every-

Lindbergh's Triangle Encounter

Aviator Charles Lindbergh reportedly encountered an unexplained haze and compass abnormalities while flying his famous plane the _Spirit of St. Louis_ through the Bermuda Triangle in 1928.

Charles Lindbergh flew the _Spirit of St. Louis_ through the Bermuda Triangle.

thing else was yellow mud."[17] Once inside this foggy haze, Caidin said, the plane's compass whirled around and all the sophisticated electronic equipment aboard the plane began to fail. After a while, he navigated his way out of the fog and the electronics began functioning normally again.

Author Bruce Gernon experienced a similar occurrence near Andros, an island of the Bahamas in December 1970. Gernon and his father nervously flew through an odd cloud formation that made it appear as if they were flying through a tunnel. Gernon reported that once they were out of the cloud tunnel, the plane was surrounded by a "dull grayish white haze."[18] As with Caidin's experience, all of Gernon's electronic and navigational equipment malfunctioned. When the haze finally broke, the equipment returned to normal. Gernon has never forgotten his brush with the mysteries of the Bermuda Triangle. He is convinced that something he calls an "electronic fog" is responsible for many of the accidents that occur in the Triangle.

Chapter 4

Bermuda Triangle Theories

ossible explanations for the disappearing ships
and planes, the fog and mist, and the numerous unexplainable happenings that plague the
area of the Bermuda Triangle are widely debated.
Some researchers believe that these occurrences are no
more frequent in the Bermuda Triangle than in other
large areas of well-traveled ocean in other parts of the
world. Others think that a greater number of accidents and unusual disappearances occur in the
Bermuda Triangle than in other geographical areas.
While many feel that the majority of the losses in the
Triangle can be explained in ways that are not at all
mysterious, their opponents firmly believe a supernatural cause is the only explanation.

Explanations for Bermuda Triangle accidents include human error and mechanical failure.

Human Error and Mechanical Failure

Of the widely varying theories that have been suggested regarding the fate of the ships, planes, and passengers lost in the Bermuda Triangle, the most obvious theory is simply that the losses were accidental. As with all people, aircraft pilots and ship captains are not perfect. Human error may be the reason for many of these accidents. A ship can be damaged in an underwater collision, or it can be capsized by shifting cargo. Aircraft pilots sometimes veer off course or run out of fuel. Unfortunately for those involved, no matter what precautions are taken, accidents are sometimes unavoidable.

In some cases, poor plane or ship maintenance or mechanical failure can produce serious consequences for pilots and captains. If a plane or ship is not taken care of properly, accidents can happen. Ships that are in bad repair have been known to break apart when they encounter rough seas. Planes may crash due to engine failure or malfunction. Leaking fuel tanks can cause fires or explosions on both planes and ships. Since some of the deepest underwater trenches in the world are found beneath the waters of the Bermuda Triangle, ships and planes that appear to have disappeared without a trace may have simply settled into these great depths.

Lightning and other weather phenomena have been given as explanations for Bermuda Triangle disappearances.

Environmental Factors

Weather-related explanations are often the first theories brought forth in Bermuda Triangle investigations. Weather conditions on the ocean can be **volatile** and rapidly changing. Thunderstorms, lightning, and hurricanes can all wreak havoc with the ships on the sea and the planes that fly above it. The fierce winds of hurricanes and strong storms can create waves so huge that they can sink ships. Storms and hurricanes can also cause **downdrafts**, strong downward currents of air that are known to be factors in some plane crashes. Waterspouts, tornadoes that form over water, can also form during thunderstorms and cause deadly accidents on the sea.

Lightning can trigger explosions aboard a ship or aircraft if the strike is located near a fuel tank. Lightning is also known to disrupt sensitive electronic equipment such as compasses and radios. One rare form of lightning, called **ball lightning**, could explain some of the odd glowing lights seen in the area of the Bermuda Triangle. Ball lightning has been described as a baseball to basketball-size glowing light that moves sideways through the air before or during a thunderstorm. This may be what Christopher Columbus saw shoot across the sky in his travels within the Triangle.

Along with storms, huge waves called **rogue waves** have also been connected to disasters in the Bermuda Triangle. These giant waves, sometimes

Monster Waves

A 2004 study examined satellite data and discovered that rogue waves occur much more frequently than scientists first believed. These giant waves, some as tall as a ten-story building, can easily damage or destroy the ships that encounter them.

called freak waves, can rise to heights of over 100 feet (30m) and capsize ships. These waves can form from undersea earthquakes, landslides, volcanic eruptions, or when normal waves meet strong ocean currents.

One of the most recent studies of ship loss in the Bermuda Triangle led to an interesting discovery. Some scientists suggest pockets of underwater methane gas might be to blame. According to researchers, methane, a colorless, odorless gas, bubbles up from the ocean's floor beneath the Bermuda Triangle. If enough gas is generated and a large amount of bubbles reach the ocean's surface, a ship could sink because the bubbles would not be able to keep the ship afloat. Geologist Bill Dillon had this to say about the discovery: "There's no doubt that methane bubbles could sink a ship. There's evidence to prove it. On several occasions,

Some of the Bermuda Triangle's many mysteries have been blamed on the presence of UFOs.

oil drilling rigs have sunk as the result of [methane] gas escape."[19]

Theories of the Supernatural

Not everyone believes that human error, mechanical failure, or environmental conditions is to blame for the occurrences in the Bermuda Triangle. Some feel strongly that there are many more mysterious explanations that only **paranormal** study can uncover.

Alien abductions and the presence of UFOs is one popular theory put forth by those who believe the paranormal plays a role in the Bermuda Triangle disappearances. One report relates a high number of UFO sightings within the area of the Bermuda Triangle. Some people feel there is only one way to explain the mystery of ships, planes, and people vanishing without a trace. They believe that these vessels and their passengers and crews were carried off by alien beings from other worlds. Since

Volcanic eruptions, tidal waves, and the lost city of Atlantis have all been linked to the Bermuda Triangle.

it is difficult to gather concrete evidence in reported cases of UFO sightings and possible alien abductions, many people dismiss these explanations as fantastical nonsense, but others stand by their belief that this is the only possible explanation.

Other popular supernatural theories include time warps, black holes, and interference from an ancient lost world. A few pilots who have encountered unusual circumstances in the Bermuda Triangle tell stories of strange time differences while flying through the area. Pilot Bruce Gernon reported his plane arrived at its destination 30 minutes earlier than it should have. He stated there was no possible way his aircraft could have flown at the speed necessary to arrive that early. Gernon and others are convinced they experienced a time warp while flying through the Triangle. Time warps are said to be areas where the normal flow of time is disrupted.

Loss of ships and planes through black holes are another theory suggested by some paranormal researchers. Black holes are formed in space when stars collapse. Black holes have an enormous pull of gravity and if any matter enters the hole, it cannot escape. Some people believe that an unknown force may have pulled ships, planes, and their occupants from their locations in the Bermuda Triangle into black holes. Scientists agree that black holes exist in space, but most remain unconvinced that black holes have any connection to Bermuda Triangle disappearances.

Other people look to the ancient past for their explanations of events in the Bermuda Triangle. Thousands of years ago, stories were written of a strong and impressive empire called Atlantis. According to legend, the island of Atlantis was swallowed up by the Atlantic Ocean around 9500 B.C. Author Charles Berlitz and others believe what is now called the Lost City of Atlantis lies on the ocean floor beneath the Bermuda Triangle. Berlitz has speculated that the underwater city of Atlantis, with its amazingly advanced technology, could still be active and could be responsible for the disappearances in the Triangle.

No single explanation exists for the causes of the numerous losses that have occurred in the Bermuda Triangle. Debate will continue as scientists, paranormal

Studying the Triangle

Aboard one of the largest cruise ships in the world exists a state-of-the-art laboratory that helps scientists better understand the sea. On its weekly Caribbean cruises, the Ocean Lab measures water temperatures, current speeds, and weather conditions to learn more about the Bermuda Triangle and other ocean areas.

researchers, survivors, and the loved ones of those lost work to determine the actual circumstances surrounding these unusual events. Widely ranging opinions on these tragedies and the continuing loss of life in the area will ensure that the mystery of the Bermuda Triangle will live on. An oceanographer from the University of Miami, Hans Graber says, "Science can explain some things that happen in the Bermuda Triangle. But there will always remain some mystery or mysterious events that even science cannot explain."[20]

Notes

Chapter 1: What Is the Bermuda Triangle?

1. Quoted in Gian J. Quasar, *Into the Bermuda Triangle: Pursuing the Truth Behind the World's Greatest Mystery*. Camden, ME: International Marine/McGraw-Hill, 2004, pp. 113–14.

2. Quoted in Quasar, *Into the Bermuda Triangle*, p. 115.

3. Charles Berlitz, *The Bermuda Triangle: An Incredible Saga of Unexplained Disappearances*. New York: Doubleday, 1974, p. 60.

4. Quoted in Rob MacGregor and Bruce Gernon, *The Fog: A Never Before Published Theory of the Bermuda Triangle Phenomenon*. Woodbury, MN: Llewellyn, 2005, pp. 44–45.

5. U.S. Coast Guard, "FAQs from the Historians Office," www.uscg.mil/hq/g-cp/history/faqs/triangle.html.

Chapter 2: Vanishing Ships and Crews

6. Quoted in Larry Kusche, *The Bermuda Triangle: Mystery Solved*. Amherst, NY: Prometheus, 1986, p. 54.

7. Quoted in Kusche, *The Bermuda Triangle*, p. 54.

8. Quoted in Quasar, *Into the Bermuda Triangle*, p. 100.

9. Quoted in Quasar, *Into the Bermuda Triangle*, p. 101.

10. Quoted in Quasar, *Into the Bermuda Triangle*, p. 102.

Chapter 3: Disappearing Planes

11. Quoted in Quasar, *Into the Bermuda Triangle*, p. 43.
12. Quoted in Michael McDonell, "Lost Patrol," *Naval Aviation News*, June 1973, pp. 8–16.
13. Quoted in McDonell, "Lost Patrol," pp. 8-16.
14. Quoted in Vincent H. Gaddis, "The Deadly Bermuda Triangle," *Argosy*, February 1964, pp. 28–29, 116–18.
15. Quoted in Berlitz, *The Bermuda Triangle*, p. 23.
16. Quoted in Meg Jones, "Bermuda Triangle Mystery Still Haunts," *Milwaukee Journal Sentinel*, December 17, 2005.
17. Quoted in Quasar, *Into the Bermuda Triangle*, p. 104.
18. Quoted in Quasar, *Into the Bermuda Triangle*, p. 110.

Chapter 4: Bermuda Triangle Theories

19. Quoted in Rene Ebersole, "Bubble Trouble," *Current Science*, November 2001, p. 10.
20. Quoted in MacGregor and Gernon, *The Fog*, p. 89.

Glossary

ball lightning: A glowing ball of light that moves sideways through the air, sometimes associated with thunderstorms.

derelicts: Ships that have been abandoned or deserted.

downdrafts: Strong downward air currents usually associated with thunderstorms.

global positioning system (GPS): A tool that can exactly pinpoint the location of an object on Earth through the use of satellite signals.

mayday: An internationally recognized distress call often used by ships and aircraft.

paranormal: Something that is impossible to explain scientifically.

phenomena: Occurrences that are out of the ordinary.

rogue waves: Extremely large, unpredictable ocean waves that form without warning.

SOS: A call or radio signal used by ships and aircraft in serious distress.

superstitious: Believing something because of ignorance or fear of the unknown.

volatile: To become suddenly violent or dangerous.

waterspouts: Tornadoes that extend from the ocean's surface up to the cloud base.

zooplankton: Plankton that is made up of microscopic animals.

For Further Exploration

Books

Nathan Aaseng, *The Bermuda Triangle*. San Diego: Lucent, 2001. This book provides an overview of the mysteries and theories surrounding the Bermuda Triangle.

Chris Oxlade, *Can Science Solve It? The Mystery of the Bermuda Triangle*. Chicago, IL: Heinemann Library, 2000. This easy-to-read book covers all the basics of the Bermuda Triangle and includes an extensive glossary.

David West and Mike Lacey, *The Bermuda Triangle: Strange Happenings at Sea*. New York: Rosen, 2006. Explore the mysteries of the Bermuda Triangle in this graphic novel format.

DVDs

Decoding the Past: Mysteries of the Bermuda Triangle. A&E Television, 2007. This DVD produced by the History Channel investigates several disasters that have occurred in the Bermuda Triangle and offers various theories about them.

Web Sites

The Bermuda Triangle. (www.bermuda-triangle.org). This Web site is maintained by Gian J. Quasar, author of *Into the Bermuda Triangle: Pursuing the Truth Behind the World's Greatest*

Mystery. Quasar is considered one of the top authorities on the Triangle.

Explorer of the Seas. (www.rsmas.miami.edu/rccl/passengers-faq.html). To learn more about ocean and atmospheric research that is being conducted by Ocean Lab on the cruise ship *Explorer of the Seas*, check out this Web site.

U.S. Navy Historical Center. (www.history.navy.mil/faqs/faq8-1.htm). Articles including information about the USS *Cyclops*, the TBM Avengers (flight 19), and other issues regarding the Bermuda Triangle can be found on this site.

Index

Picture Credits

About the Author

Katy S. Duffield is the author of a children's picture book, *Farmer McPeepers and His Missing Milk Cows,* and she has written for many children's magazines. Duffield has also written two other books for KidHaven Press—*Poltergeists* and *Ken Kutaragi: PlayStation Developer.* For more information, visit her Web site at www.katyduffield.com.